Mosquito One

Mosquito One

Text Copyright © 2020 Blue Tang Ltd
Illustrations Copyright © 2020 Blue Tang Ltd

This book is sold subject to the condition that it shall not, by way of trade or otherwise, be lent, re-sold, hired out, or otherwise circulated without the publisher's prior consent in any form of binding or cover other than that in which it is published and without a similar condition including this condition being imposed on the subsequent purchaser.

All rights reserved. No part of this publication may be reproduced or distributed in any form or by any means, electronic or mechanical, including photocopying, recording, or any information storage and retrieval system, without permission in writing from the publisher.

ISBN: 978-1-927395-96-7

Copyright © 2020 by Blue Tang Ltd., and Published by Guava Press, an imprint of Blue Tang Ltd.
Book Design by Nitya George
Guava Press™ is a Trademark of Blue Tang Ltd.
Guava Press, Blue Tang Ltd., Newmarket, ON L3X 2R6, Canada
ISBN 978-1-927395-96-7
Printed in India

Mosquito One

Adapted from a traditional Jamaican rhyme

Written by **Al Campbell**
Illustrated by **Nitya George**

Mosquito one, mosquito two.
Mosquitoes jump in the hot callaloo.

Mosquito one, mosquito two.
Mosquitoes jump in the Dutch pot too.

Mosquito one, mosquito two.
Mosquitoes jump in the big pot of stew.

Mosquito one, mosquito two.

Mosquitoes jump in Mama's new hairdo.

Mosquito one, mosquito two.

Mosquitoes make Papa lose a screw.

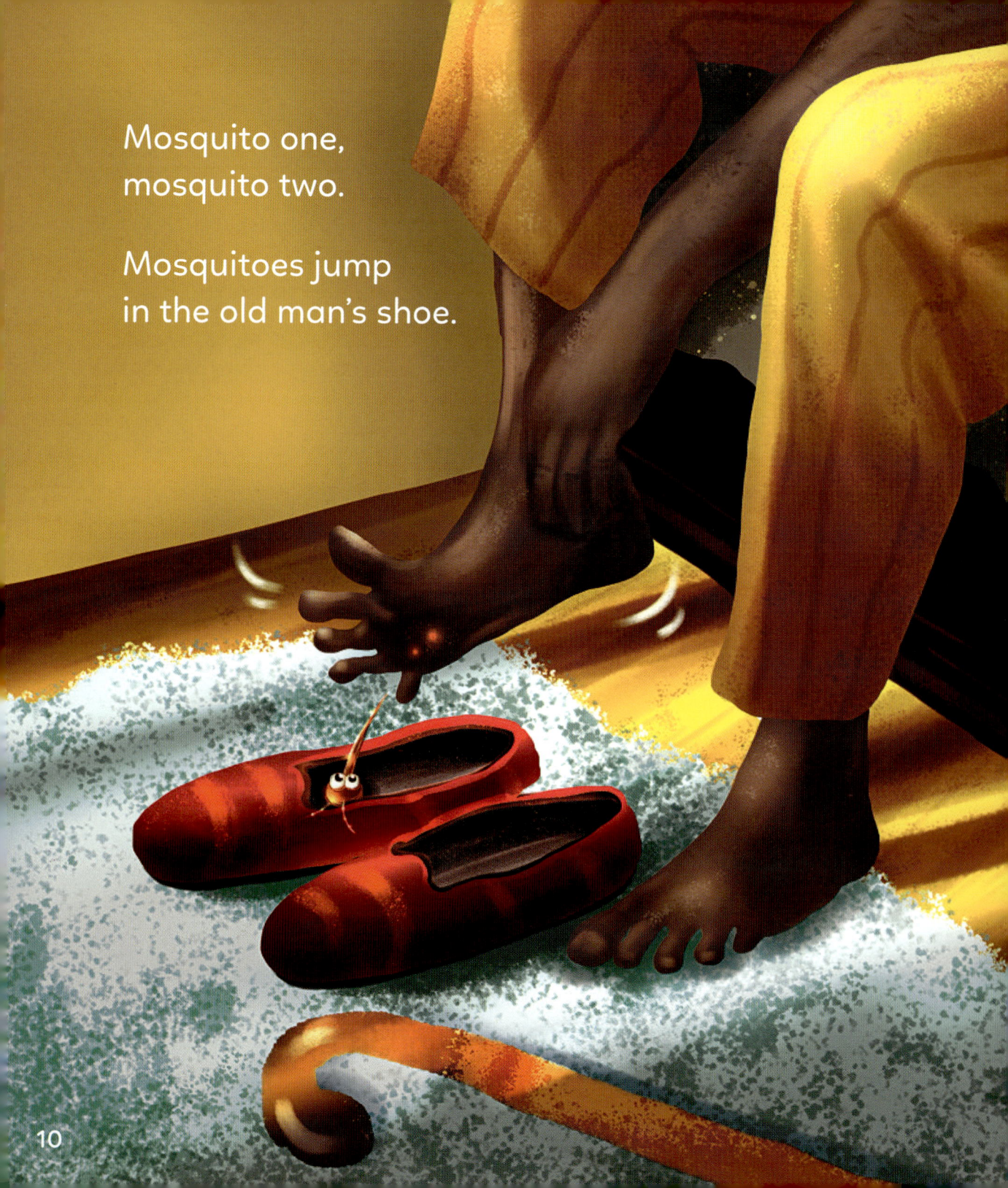

Mosquito one, mosquito two.

Mosquitoes jump in the old man's shoe.

Mosquito one, mosquito two.
Mosquitoes make Johnny run out of the loo.

Mosquito one, mosquito two.

Mosquitoes bit three little monkeys in the zoo.

Mosquito one, mosquito two.

Mosquitoes like to hide in thick bamboo.

Mosquito one, mosquito two.
Mosquitoes come when the sky is not blue.

Mosquito one, mosquito two.

Mosquitoes are not afraid of me or you.

Mosquito three, mosquito four.

Mosquito time you'd better close your door.

Mosquito five, mosquito six.
Mosquito bites itch more than cowitch.

Mosquito seven, mosquito eight.

Mosquitoes come inside if you close too late.

Mosquito nine, mosquito ten.

Mosquitoes make you curse again and again.

So remember mosquito one, mosquito two.
Mosquitoes like blood that is new-new-new.

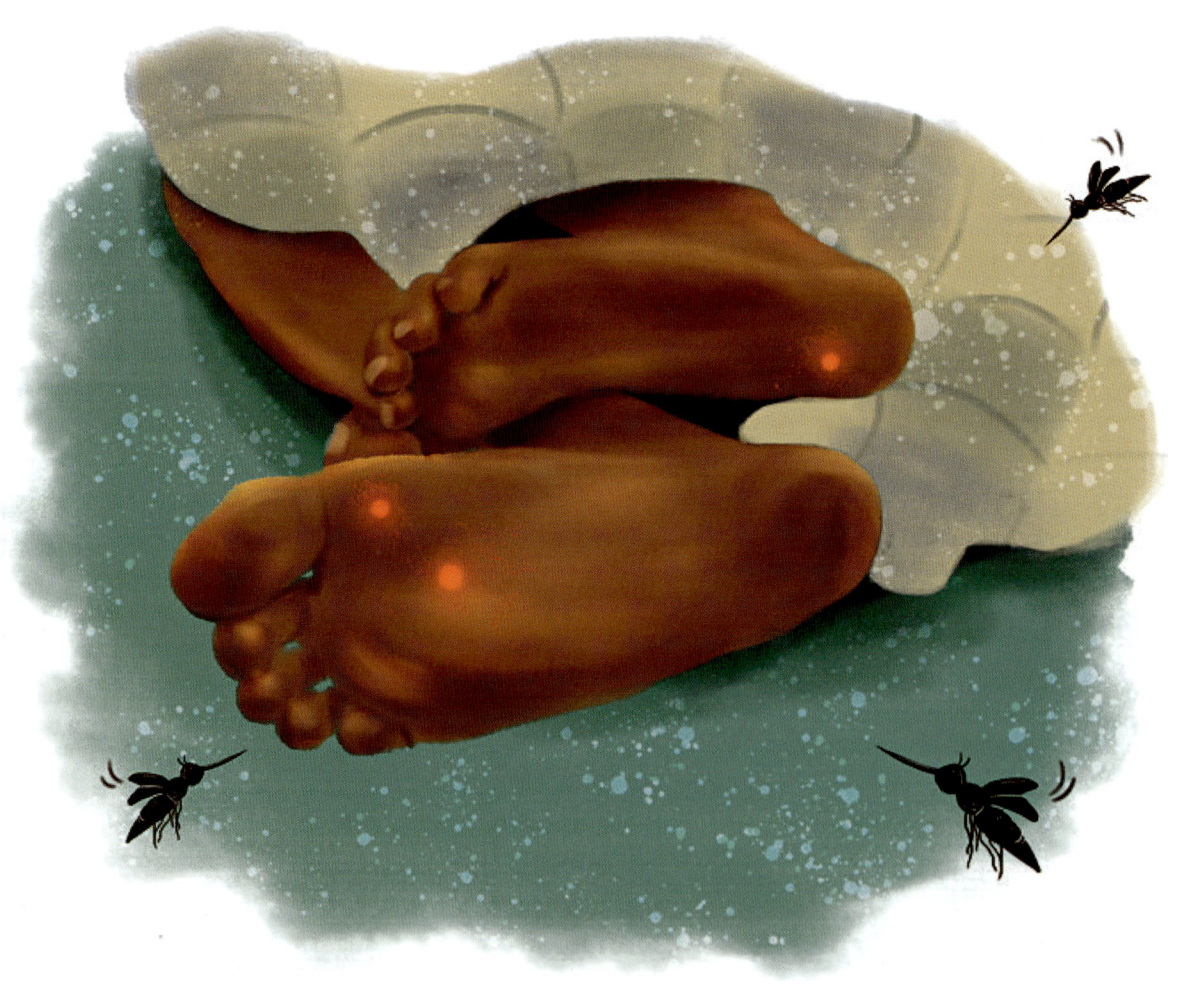

Mosquito One

Mosquito one, mosquito two.
Mosquitoes jump in the hot callaloo.

Mosquito one, mosquito two.
Mosquitoes jump in the old man's shoe.

Mosquito one, mosquito two.
Mosquitoes jump in the Dutch pot too.

Baby can't walk, baby can't talk.
Baby can't eat with a knife and fork.

Mosquitoes are Insects

A mosquito is an insect. Each one has three basic body parts: head, thorax, and abdomen.

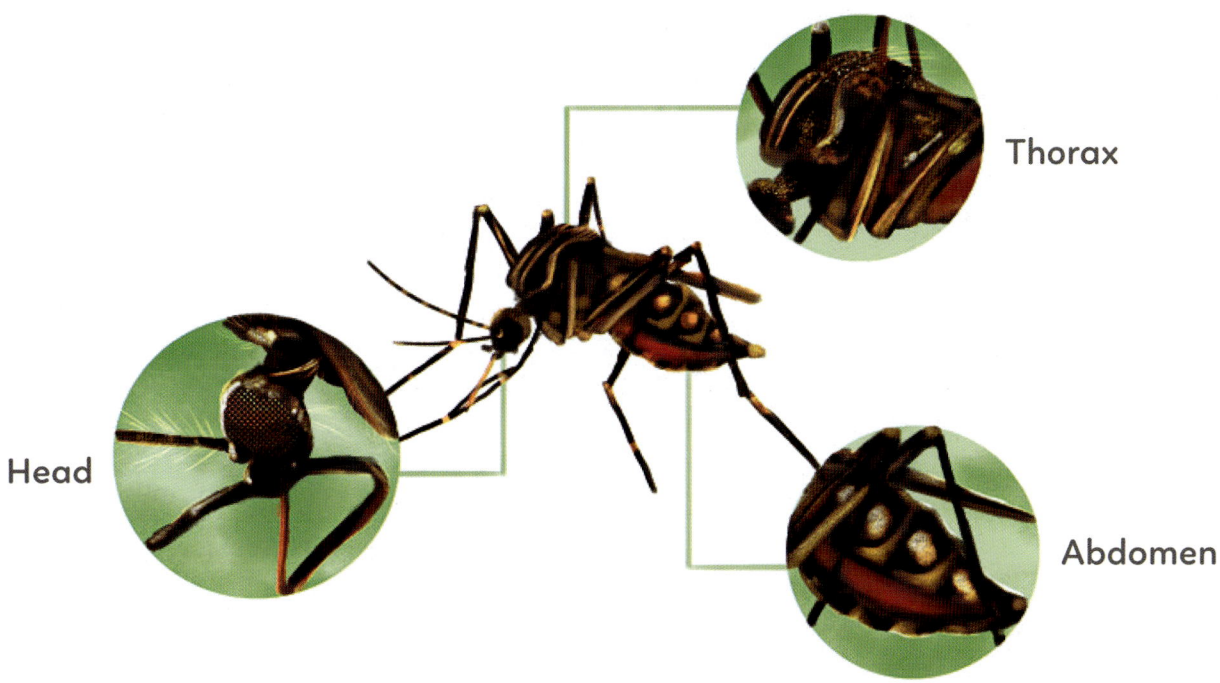

The head has two eyes, antennae for sensors, and a mouth.

The thorax is where the two wings and six legs are attached. It also contains the heart.

The abdomen contains the digestive and excretory organs.

Mosquitoes

There are over **3,000** mosquito species in the world. Most mosquitoes are harmless to humans as they feed only on snakes, frogs, birds, and other animals.

There are however other mosquitoes, like the **AEDES AEGYPTI,** who prefer to feed on cows, horses, and people. That is why mosquitoes spread some of the world's worst diseases, including malaria, yellow fever, Zika, Chikungunya, encephalitis, West Nile virus, and dengue.

Many people have asked the question, are mosquitoes necessary? Why don't we kill them all and wipe them off the face of the Earth?

The simple answer is that mosquitoes actually serve many useful purposes. Here are a few:

Mosquitoes

- Mosquitoes are an important food source for many animals such as fish, turtles, dragonflies, birds, and bats.

- Mosquitoes are important pollinators for plants such as some herbs and orchids.

- The chemicals in a mosquito's mouth are useful to make medicine. The chemicals are natural anticoagulants that help to prevent blood clots. Anticoagulants help to prevent or treat life-threatening conditions such as deep vein thrombosis, pulmonary embolism, and stroke.

- Humans need to learn to live in harmony with mosquitoes. Maybe a better way is to try to prevent our exposure to mosquitoes.

Ten Facts About Mosquitoes

- Only female mosquitoes actually "bite" animals and drink blood.
- Male mosquitoes only feed on plant juices.
- A mosquito's wings beat about 1,000 times per second.
- The life cycle of a mosquito is: egg - larva - pupa - adult stages.
- Most female mosquitoes lay up to 200 eggs at a time.
- The scientific name for mosquitoes is Culicidae.
- Mosquitoes are invertebrates (animals without backbones).
- A group of mosquitoes is called a "Swarm."
- The average life span of a mosquito is 2 weeks to 6 months.
- Mosquitoes can drink 3 times their own body weight in blood.